The Science of Living Things

What are Camouflage and Mimicry?

Bobbie Kalman & John Crossingham

 Crabtree Publishing Company

www.crabtreebooks.com

The Science of Living Things Series
A Bobbie Kalman Book

(Dedicated by John Crossingham)
To Scottie Remila - a master of disguise and illusion

Editor-in-Chief
Bobbie Kalman

Writing team
Bobbie Kalman
John Crossingham

Editors
Kate Calder
Amanda Bishop

Copy editors
Kathryn Smithyman
Heather Fitzpatrick

Computer design
Kymberley McKee Murphy

Production coordinator
Heather Fitzpatrick

Photo researcher
John Crossingham

Consultant
Patricia Loesche, Ph.D., Animal Behavior
Program, Department of Psychology,
University of Washington

Photographs
Frank Balthis: pages 21 (top), 25 (bottom left)
Robert McCaw: pages 5, 6 (right), 12 (both), 19 (bottom),
    25 (top), 29 (top)
Allen Blake Sheldon: page 30
Tom Stack & Associates: David B. Fleetham: pages 10 (bottom), 16;
    Thomas Kitchin: page 9 (top); Kitchin and Hurst: page 23 (top);
    Joe McDonald: pages 7 (top left), 18, 22 (top), 27 (top);
    Randy Morse: page 14;
    Brian Parker: pages 21 (bottom), 31;
    Milton Rand: page 28;
    Mike Severens: page 23 (bottom);
    Tom & Therisa Stack: page 26 (bottom left)
Michael Turco: pages 7 (top right), 8, 26 (top and bottom right),
    29 (bottom)
Other images by Adobe Image Library and Digital Stock

Illustrations
All illustrations by Margaret Amy Reiach

Separations and film
Embassy Graphics

Printer
Worzalla Publishing

Crabtree Publishing Company

www.crabtreebooks.com   1-800-387-7650

PMB16A
350 Fifth Avenue
Suite 3308
New York, NY
10118

612 Welland Avenue
St. Catharines
Ontario
Canada
L2M 5V6

73 Lime Walk
Headington
Oxford
OX3 7AD
United Kingdom

Cataloging in Publication Data
Kalman, Bobbie
    What are camouflage and mimicry?
        p. cm. -- (The Science of living things)
        Includes index.
    ISBN 0-86505-985-3 (RLB) ISBN 0-86505-962-4 (pbk.)
    This book introduces children to ways in which animals hide to
avoid predators or hunt prey.
    1. Camouflage (Biology)—Juvenile literature. 2. Mimicry
(Biology)—Juvenile literature. [1. Camouflage (Biology) 2. Mimicry
(Biology)] I. Crossingham, John. II. Title. III. Series: Kalman, Bobbie.
Science of living things.
    QL759.K35 2001
    591.47'2—dc21

                                                    LC00-069365
                                                    CIP

Contents

Everybody hide

In order to survive, many animals use **camouflage** to find food or hide from their natural enemies. Camouflage is a color or pattern on an animal's body that allows it to blend in with a certain background. When an animal using camouflage is not moving, it is difficult for other animals to see it.

For hunters and hunted

An animal that hunts other animals is called a **predator**. The animals that a predator hunts are called **prey**. Many animals use camouflage so predators will not see or eat them. Predators also use camouflage to sneak up on their prey.

Copycats

Some animals take camouflage one step further. These animals do more than just blend into a background—they look like something they are not. This ability to copy is called **mimicry**. Animals that use mimicry protect themselves by looking like a rock, plant, or even bird droppings!

(left) By staying still, this brown and white owl is camouflaged by the branches as it watches for prey.

This white-tailed deer is well hidden in this forest. Its brown coat and white markings blend in with the trees and snow.

Many shades

The type of camouflage an animal uses depends on the environment in which it is hiding. Many animals stay unseen by having a single body color. Some have several colors with patterns and markings. Other animals are able to change their color to blend in with their surroundings.

Single tone

The most basic form of camouflage is using a single color. This color is usually one that is common in nature, such as green or brown. The animal "disappears" against a background of the same color.

See spot hide

Spots and stripes on an animal confuse predators. These markings can look like shadows or grass and hide the animal's body. This thirteen-lined ground squirrel blends in with the grasses around it.

Shade shifters

Some animals can actually change their body color to match their environment. This leaf-tailed gecko can alter its color to match many background shades. Its color depends on the color of the tree on which it is resting.

Brilliant disguise

Many animals that use mimicry have changed over time to look like a part of their environment. The katydid's wings (below) resemble a leaf on the forest floor. The leafy sea dragon (bottom) has growths that look like seaweed.

Part of the scenery

Many animals use a single color to blend in with their environment. Green or brown snakes are well hidden in trees and on the forest floor. Brown bears are camouflaged against tree trunks. Frogs are the same color as water plants. Rainforest reptiles, such as the anole lizard shown above, are often green to blend in with the leaves of plants. Grassland and prairie animals are shades of brown like the tan grasses of their home. Both prey animals, such as prairie dogs, and predators, such as mighty lions, have brown coloring.

Winter wonderland

In areas with a lot of snow year round, many animals are completely white. Arctic foxes, polar bears, and snowy owls all have a white coat. Some animals that live in areas with cold winters and warm summers have coats that change with the seasons. In summer, the arctic hare and the ptarmigan are brownish-gray. Once the snow arrives, however, their fur or feathers change to pure white.

From the frozen Arctic to the hot African grasslands, predators use a single-colored coat to hide from prey.

Two tones

Having a light-colored breast allows birds such as this tern to sneak up on prey below.

Animals that spend their time in water or high in the air have different camouflage needs than those of land animals. Their enemies can see them from both above and below. Many fish and birds have two tones—a dark-colored top and a light-colored underside.

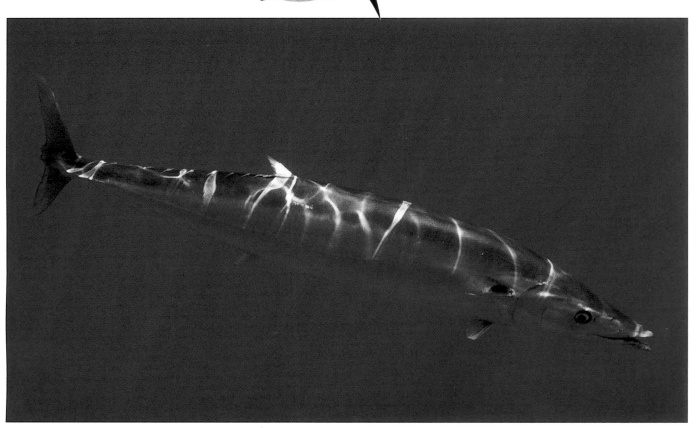

This wahoo fish shows how two-tone camouflage can make a fish appear thin and hidden.

Undercover underwater

From underneath, the surface of water looks bright because the sun is shining down through it. When looking up at a fish, its shimmering silvery underside blends in with the bright surface. The ocean depths, however, look almost black. When looking down at the same fish, its dark blue top matches the black depths.

This two-tone camouflage also works for birds in the air. When looking down on a bird with a dark top, it is difficult to spot the bird against the dark ground. Meanwhile, animals looking up at a bird with a light belly are unable to spot the bird in the bright sky.

Although penguins are easy to see on land, their dark back and light belly hide them well underwater.

Seeing spots

Many animals have added spots and stripes to their camouflage. Animals are recognized by the shape of their body. Spots, stripes, and other markings break up the outline of an animal's body. For example, the speckles of dark color on the grasshopper shown above, make its outline difficult to see against the gravel.

Shadows through the trees

Many animals with spots and stripes live in forests or grasslands. As sunlight shines between the trees and tall grass, the plants leave long shadows on the ground. An animal's stripes look like these shadows.

When the American bittern is afraid, it stretches its neck upwards. Its beak and stripes help blend in with the grass. If the wind is blowing, the bird sways back and forth to imitate the breeze.

Put on your coat

Certain species of **mollusks** have a spotted skin that they can take on and off like a coat. The soft bodies of most mollusks, such as clams and scallops, are covered by hard shells. Although these shells offer protection, they are easy to see. Some mollusks, however, use a second skin called a **cloak** to cover their shell. When the mollusk wants to hide, it can slowly cover itself with the cloak. The cloak is marked with a random pattern of shapes or stripes. This pattern makes it difficult for a predator to see the mollusk clearly.

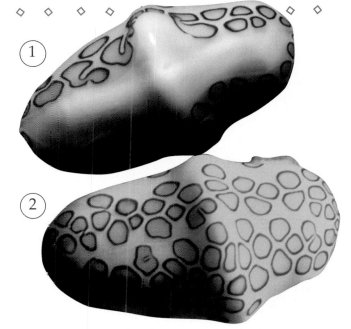

1. The mollusk slowly moves its cloak over its plain shell until...
2. ...it is completely covered with spots!

Sometimes an animal's stripes help it blend in with other animals. These fish are easy to see on their own. In a large group, however, their stripes make it difficult to single out one fish. A predator can become confused by the stripes, giving the fish more time to escape.

Eye spy

The eyes are often the first thing that gives a hidden animal away. Even well camouflaged animals such as polar bears have eyes that are easy to see. In addition, many predators attack the head and neck of their prey to kill the animal. A few animals have specialized spots and stripes that hide their eyes and head from their enemies.

Some fish, such as the butterfly fish shown above, have a stripe across their eyes. The stripe disguises the eyeball, making it difficult to spot. This fish also has a false **eyespot** near its tail, distracting predators into thinking that the fish's tail is its head. As the predator lunges to bite the "head," the fish swims away and escapes!

Boo!

Eyespots fool predators into believing that an animal is bigger than it actually is. Moths are usually well camouflaged against trees by their color, but many moths also have eyespots for added protection. When a moth is startled, it spreads its wings quickly to flash its large eyespots. The predator is briefly frightened by this sudden motion, and the moth is able to fly away.

This moth's four large eyespots can startle its predators.

Caterpillars are slow moving and often rely on camouflage and mimicry to survive. This caterpillar's eyespots and large red horns make it seem fierce.

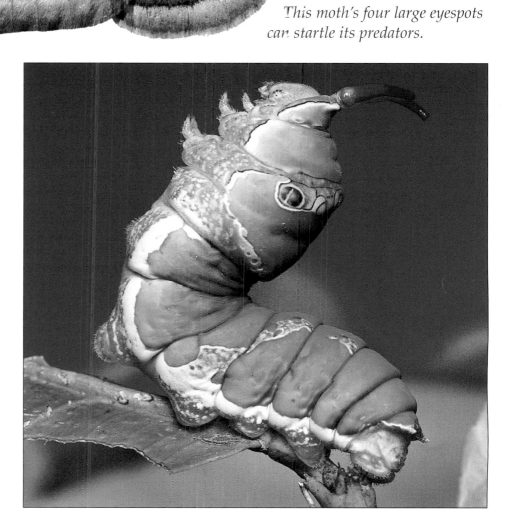

I'm looking through you!

Have you ever wanted to be invisible? A few animals
have developed body parts that are **transparent**,
or see-through. The parts that are transparent
cannot be seen against the color of
the background of their home.

*This tiny transparent shrimp is
floating among the tentacles of a sea
anemone. Its body has been changed
so that it is almost invisible.*

Looking glass

The amazing glass frog, shown right, is nearly transparent. When lying on a leaf, it seems to disappear. Only the frog's internal organs and eyes are visible. The green spots that cover the frog's back hide these body parts.

Phantom limb

Some insects have limbs that are transparent. Normally, a grasshopper's long legs are easy to see and can ruin the animal's camouflage. A few grasshoppers have legs that are clear, although their body is green or brown.

This grasshopper's clear legs and antennae make it look more like a dying leaf than an insect.

Changing colors

Most animals that use camouflage are able to hide in only one environment. For example, a polar bear is easy to see if there is no snow! There are a few animals, however, that can change their colors to blend in with almost any environment. These masters of disguise are some of the best-camouflaged animals in the animal kingdom.

The chameleon

The most famous color changer is the chameleon. Underneath its transparent skin are layers of different-colored cells. The colors include yellow, red, and blue. The chameleon changes colors by making the cells smaller or larger. For example, to turn green, its yellow and blue cells become larger.

The octopus

Many sea animals such as fish and seahorses can also change color to hide from enemies. The octopus has skin that is full of **pigment**, which is a colored liquid. It uses this pigment to blend into different areas on the sea floor. By changing the amount of pigment in its skin, the octopus becomes lighter or darker. It can even add more pigment to certain areas of its skin and give itself spots or stripes.

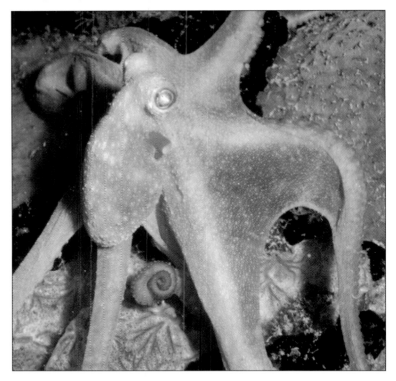

The crab spider can quickly change the amount of pigment in its body to match the flowers nearby. It is almost invisible as it waits to catch unsuspecting insects.

Made for hiding

Camouflage can be more than just fancy colors and stripes. Some animals rely more on their body's shape to help them hide. Using their well-adapted eyes and nostrils, they can hide most of their body underwater or underground and still breathe and watch out for enemies or prey.

Hide and go eat!

The frog shown above has eyes that are raised higher on its head. This position and its green coloring allow it to hide in shallow water and wait for prey such as insects. When its prey is in range, the frog quickly flicks out its long tongue and catches the insect.

Bury me in the sand

Many land and sea animals bury themselves in the sand to hide from predators and prey. Certain crabs and desert snakes wriggle underneath a thin layer of sand. The flounder is a fish with a remarkable body! Baby flounder look like normal fish but as they grow, one of their eyes moves slowly until both eyes are on one side of their head. To hide, the flounder lies on the ocean floor on its side. It shakes and covers itself with sand until only its eyes are showing.

The ghost crab can dig itself into the sand with only its tall eyes exposed.

(above) Although this flounder is perfectly hidden, it can still look out for approaching prey or danger.

Stay away!

If so many animals survive by using dull colors to hide, why do brightly colored animals exist? Usually animals with bright markings are trying to warn their enemies that they are dangerous. Many of these animals are poisonous or have bad-tasting flesh. Their bright markings warn predators, "Leave me alone—I am not good to eat."

(left) Monarch butterflies have a foul, bitter taste that most predators do not like. Their striking wings warn their enemies that they are in for a bitter experience!

Reds and yellows

Animals that are poisonous use shades of red and yellow as warning colors. The highly poisonous coral snake, shown on the opposite page, has large bands of red and yellow along its body. These colors stand out against the greens and browns usually found in nature, so they are like warning signs.

(right) The many species of South American poison arrow frogs are the most poisonous animals in the world. This pair's bright stripes give a clear warning!

Nudibranch, or sea slugs, release a poison when they are attacked. They come in several warning colors such as yellow and orange.

Look at me!

Another reason for animals to be seen rather than hidden is to **mate**, or make babies. In order to mate, a male animal must attract a female. Females seek out the healthiest males as their partners, so their babies will be healthy. Many males use bright colors to let their partners know that they are available to mate.

Bright birds

Male birds are well-known for having bright colors to attract a female. Many male birds are much more colorful than the females of their species. They parade in front of a female and try to win her attention. Some of these birds have bright crests or feathers that grow only during the mating season.

Face mask

Male animals often have to fight with one another for a female. Some males use color to scare other males away and impress the females. The mandrill baboon, shown bottom right, has bright blue and red markings on its face. These colors attract females and frighten predators.

The puffin's attractive beak is most colorful during mating season.

The male frigate bird has a bright red chest sac that it can inflate when it wants to impress a female.

Pl nt, rock, or nimal?

Every part of an animal that uses mimicry is special because it looks like something else. Many animals that mimic look like plants or rocks. The predators of these animals are not interested in these things, so they leave the animal alone.

(left) When slender stick insects stay still in a tree, it is almost impossible to tell them apart from the branches. Can you find this stick insect?

*This sargassum nudibranch has growths on its body and colors that are similar to those found on **sargassum**. Sargassum is a type of seaweed.*

The caterpillar of the tiger swallowtail butterfly has markings that make it look like a bird dropping. Now that is something that no animal wants to eat!

Treehoppers are insects that have a large, curved horn on their back. This horn looks like a thorn on the plant's stem.

The sculpin is a fish that lies on the sea floor and waits for prey. It has many tiny marks and growths on its body that make it look like an algae-covered rock.

Who stole my clothes?

Not all animals that use mimicry resemble plants or rocks. Some look like other animals. They use mimicry to imitate other poisonous or dangerous animals. There are insects that pretend they are scorpions, harmless snakes that look like poisonous ones, and flies that appear to be bees! Although these animals are not poisonous themselves, predators leave them alone.

Do you think this little insect is a wasp? Guess again! The syrphid fly's bright yellow stripes look just like those found on a wasp, but this insect has no stinger.

Fooled you!

This butterfly is called a viceroy. Do you remember the foul-tasting monarch butterfly on page 22? Although this viceroy tastes good, predators also leave it alone because it looks just like a monarch butterfly.

This frog's brightly spotted skin seems to warn enemies that it is poisonous. In fact, this frog is quite harmless to predators.

Come a little closer!

Some animals have certain areas on their body for attracting attention. For example, there are lizards that have a bright tail to attract predators. This tail works like the eyespots of the butterfly fish on page 14. The predator attacks the tail and not the head, which gives the lizard a better chance to escape. Other animals use certain parts of their body as bait to fish for food.

Gone fishing

The alligator snapping turtle, shown above, lures curious prey right into its mouth. It has a thin bright-pink tongue that looks like a small worm. The turtle lies on the river bottom with its mouth wide open and its tongue out. When a small fish comes by to investigate this tasty "worm," the turtle snaps its jaws shut and catches a meal.

Flashlight fish

Some animals that live in deep or dark water are able to produce their own light. This glowing light is called **bioluminescence**. Bioluminescence is often used to catch prey. Other fish are attracted to the soft glow and swim closer. Many jellyfish, such as this one, are bioluminescent. The jellyfish also has many stinging tentacles. This sting can **paralyze**, or freeze, small fish that come too close. These curious fish are then eaten by the jellyfish.

(right) Jellyfish are some of the most beautiful animals in the sea, but it is best to watch them from a distance!

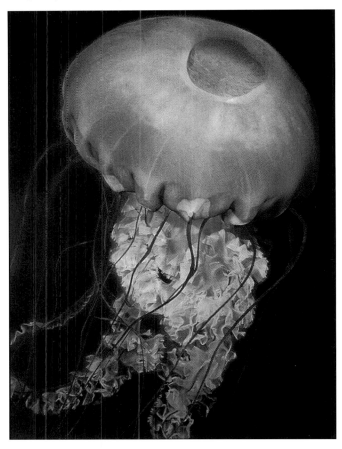

The anglerfish has a long lure on its head that hangs in front of its wide mouth. The rest of the fish is camouflaged to look like a piece of coral or rock.

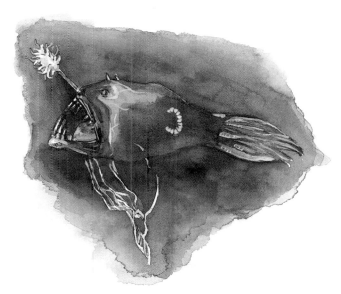

Deep sea anglerfish live in an area where little light is available. At the end of their lure is a bioluminescent bulb.

Glossary

antennae The long, sensitive feelers found on the head of some animals such as insects

bioluminescence The glow of light produced by some animals such as jellyfish and fireflies

camouflage A color pattern on an animal that allows it to hide from its enemies

cell A tiny unit that makes up all living things

crustacean Sea animals such as crabs and lobsters that have a hard exoskeleton but no backbone

eyespot A marking on an animal, which looks like an eye and confuses predators

mate To reproduce, or make babies

mimicry A color pattern or growth that makes an animal look like something else in nature

mollusks Small animals such as snails and clams, which have no backbone

nudibranch Small underwater mollusks that have no shells

paralyze To use a poison that causes an animal to lose its ability to move

pigment The material in plant and animal cells that provides color

predator An animal that hunts and eats other animals

prey An animal that is hunted and eaten by other animals

sargassum A leafy seaweed that has small, berry-like pods

transparent Describing an object that is clear and allows light to shine through it

Index

1 2 3 4 5 6 7 8 9 0   Printed in the U.S.A.   0 9 8 7 6 5 4 3 2 1